SOUTH DEVON
STEAMERS
& FERRIES

The Eddystone Lighthouse pictured from the *Waverley* on 19 May 1979. The last time I saw this view was from the deck of the GWR tender *Sir John Hawkins* in the late 1950s. Today the Eddystone is deserted – the lighthouse is automated and the steamers have all gone.

SOUTH DEVON
STEAMERS
& FERRIES

Alan Kittridge

TEMPUS

Acknowledgements

As I embark upon the task of writing the introduction and captions to these pictures, I find that I am consulting the same books and articles that have enlightened me in over twenty-five years of pursuing my interest in the west country's passenger steamers and ferries: *Westcountry Passenger Steamers* by Graham Farr (Prescot 1967); *South Coast Pleasure Steamers* by E.C.B. Thornton (Prescot 1969); *Exmouth to Starcross, an Ancient Ferry* by W.H. Rose (Exeter 1996); *Estuary & River Ferries of South West England* by Martin Langley and Edwina Small (Wolverhampton 1984); *The Fair (Few) Miles – a History of the Western Lady Ferry Service* by S.A. Armstrong; *Trip Out Guide* by Geoffrey Hamer (London, various years); *Only Brittany Ferries...* by Miles Cowsill (Kilgetty 1989). Sources and acknowledgements relating to the Dartmouth and Plymouth districts are extensive and best covered by directing the reader to: *Passenger Steamers of the River Dart & Kingsbridge Estuary* by Richard Clammer and Alan Kittridge (Truro 1987); *Passenger Steamers of the River Tamar* by Alan Kittridge (Truro 1984); and *Plymouth: Ocean Liner Port-of-Call* by Alan Kittridge (Truro 1993).

First published 2003

Tempus Publishing Limited
The Mill, Brimscombe Port,
Stroud, Gloucestershire, GL5 2QG
www.tempus-publishing.com

© Alan Kittridge, 2003

The right of Alan Kittridge to be identified as the Author
of this work has been asserted in accordance with the
Copyrights, Designs and Patents Act 1988.

British Library Cataloguing in Publication Data.
A catalogue record for this book is available from the British Library.

ISBN 0 7524 2799 7

Typesetting and origination by Tempus Publishing Limited
Printed in Great Britain by Midway Colour Print, Wiltshire

Contents

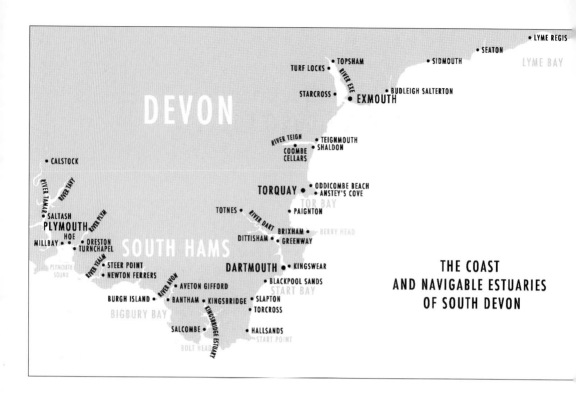

THE COAST AND NAVIGABLE ESTUARIES OF SOUTH DEVON

DEVON

LYME REGIS
SEATON
SIDMOUTH
LYME BAY
TOPSHAM
TURF LOCKS
RIVER EXE
STARCROSS
BUDLEIGH SALTERTON
EXMOUTH

CALSTOCK

RIVER TEIGN
TEIGNMOUTH
COOMBE CELLARS
SHALDON

RIVER TAVY
RIVER TAMAR

TORQUAY
ODDICOMBE BEACH
ANSTEY'S COVE
TOR BAY
PAIGNTON

RIVER PLYM
SALTASH
PLYMOUTH
HOE
MILLBAY
ORESTON
TURNCHAPEL

TOTNES
RIVER DART
DITTISHAM
BRIXHAM
GREENWAY
BERRY HEAD

SOUTH HAMS

PLYMOUTH SOUND
RIVER YEALM
STEER POINT
NEWTON FERRERS

DARTMOUTH
KINGSWEAR
BLACKPOOL SANDS
START BAY

RIVER AVON
AVETON GIFFORD
BANTHAM
KINGSBRIDGE
BURGH ISLAND
SLAPTON
TORCROSS

BIGBURY BAY

KINGSBRIDGE ESTUARY
SALCOMBE
HALLSANDS
START POINT

BOLT HEAD

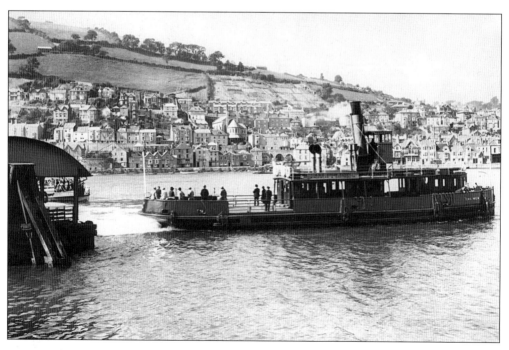

A Great Western Railway official photograph of the Kingswear Railway Ferry *The Mew* leaving Kingswear, with the bows of the River Dart Steamboat Co. Ltd paddle steamer *Kingswear Castle* behind the pontoon. Dartmouth is in the background, across the harbour.

Introduction

Few areas in England attract more holiday makers than south Devon and Cornwall. Many of these visitors have enjoyed a boat trip along the spectacular coast or up a beautiful wooded estuary, most have crossed a picturesque river or busy harbour in one of many distinctive ferries. Others live there, crossing in ferries by necessity and enjoying the same seasonal steamer trips. This collection of pictures will, hopefully, rekindle memories of steamers and ferries and introduce some lesser known, even obscure, passenger boat ventures along the south Devon coast.

From the steeply shelving shingle beaches of east Devon to the head of navigation on the River Tamar, the nature of the south Devon coast undergoes dramatic changes and has, therefore, supported a wide variety of passenger craft – many designed to operate within specific navigational environments.

The high cliffs and exposed beaches of east Devon, between Seaton and Teignmouth, don't appear to hold much promise for coastal cruising. But between the 1890s and 1930s a pair of purpose built coastal paddle steamers – the *Duchess of Devonshire* and *Duke of Devonshire* – maintained seasonal services to these and other attractions on the Devon and Dorset coasts, actually landing on the beaches. The Devon Dock, Pier & Steamship Co. Ltd of Exmouth owned and designed them. This company also owned Exmouth Docks, Exmouth Pier and Teignmouth Pier, the Starcross Ferry and operated a steamer service between Torquay and Brixham. Their coastal paddle steamers had strengthened bows to 'take' the beach and were fitted with flimsy looking, but evidently reliable, landing gear – a self contained gangplank that extended from the bow. Paddle propulsion proved ideal for their operation as the paddle wheels could be turned 'dead slow ahead', in shallow water, to hold the steamer on the beach – with a kedge anchor astern to hold her square. This risky operation was bound to end in tears, the only surprise being that it took so long. On the fateful day of 27 August 1934, the *Duchess of Devonshire* was swept broadside onto the beach at Sidmouth and stranded, never to get off. But for forty years these Exmouth based steamers provided the nicest way to visit Seaton, Beer, Sidmouth, Budleigh Salterton, Teignmouth, Torquay, Paignton, Brixham and even the beaches at Blackpool Sands, Slapton and Hallsands.

Operation of the Devon Dock, Pier & Steamship Co. Ltd's year round Starcross Ferry on the River Exe was better suited to small, shallow draught, single and twin screw steamers, built in local south Devon yards. The main purpose, in later years, of the Starcross Ferry was to link Exmouth to the Great Western Railway mainline across the River Exe. For visitors coming from the west this cut off a long journey to Exeter and a change to the London & South Western Railway (later the Southern Railway).

Torquay is arguably the only resort on south Devon's coast – it has little other purpose. As such one might expect a history of impressive pleasure steamer fleets, and if variety is the spice of your life, then Torquay's excursion opportunities would not have disappointed. Never embracing the procession of interlopers, Torquay's passenger boat operators themselves employed a succession of second-hand tonnage. Few Torquay-owned, Board of Trade-registered passenger boats were ever purpose built for the Torquay trade. The resort long suffered from lower middle class snobbery, as epitomised by the fictitious Torquay guest house owner Basil Fawlty. The char-a-banc and motor car age, however, brought in hordes of Fawlty's dreaded 'riff-raff' on day trips and during the 1950s and 1960s Torquay's passenger boat trade enjoyed its heyday, albeit largely due to more adventurous Brixham and Dartmouth interests.

The Devon Dock, Pier & Steamship Co. Ltd's steamer service across Tor Bay called for deep draught single or twin screw steamers, as crossings could get a little boisterous and deep water was always available. Since the Victorian age steamers like the *Pioneer* and the Devon Dock, Pier & Steamship Co. Ltd's *Prince Edward* provided a service for day trippers between Torquay's Princess Gardens Jetty, Paignton Promenade Pier and the New Pier at Brixham. After the Second World War this 'ferry' was revived by the Western Lady Ferry Service, which operated ex-Royal Navy Fairmile launches on the route – as they still do.

In contrast to Torquay, most of the passenger craft of the River Dart have been purpose built to operate specific routes on the river. The best known of these were the distinctive paddle steamers of the River Dart Steamboat Co. Ltd, which ran between Dartmouth and Totnes. The shape of these steamers reflected the river itself: their length was the maximum turning circle at Totnes; their depth – the water available in the river at low tide; their profusion of decks and landing platforms – the varying tidal heights at Totnes and Dartmouth; low freeboard and well decks because they never went beyond the river mouth. There were no other paddle steamers in the world like them. Fortunately one of these steamers, the *Kingswear Castle*, continues in operation, based at Chatham Historic Dockyard on the River Medway.

Similar to the River Dart, but on a smaller scale, the nearby Kingsbridge Estuary supported a succession of estuarine paddle steamers. Kingsbridge and Salcombe also maintained timetabled coastal passenger and cargo links with Plymouth – a type of service familiar on the Isles of Scilly or Lundy, perhaps, but unusual in the twentieth century on the south Devon coast.

This pictorial trip through time and south Devon ends in the Plymouth district – the largest centre of population west of Bristol. The 'Three Towns' of Plymouth, Devonport and Stonehouse once supported over thirty-five steamers serving the population of the main towns and outlying communities around the five local rivers. There were steamer services on the south Devon rivers Yealm and Plym. All of the Tamar's ferries were Cornish concerns but the east Cornwall steamer fleets depended upon and operated from landing places on the south Devon shore. River and coastal excursion passengers were drawn almost exclusively from the big local population – part of the reason that these steamers remain relatively unknown outside the area. The Saltash, Three Towns & District Steamboat Co. Ltd operated six paddle and three screw steamers in the years leading up to the First World War – all but one were purpose built for various routes on the district's waterways. The opposing Millbrook Steamboat Co. had three paddle and three screw steamers – all but one being purpose built. The sheltered navigable waters inside Plymouth Breakwater and shallow water at the heads of various navigations were ideal paddle steamer territory. Cheaper alternatives for running regular ferry services to the heads of navigation were shallow draught twin screw steamers, while deeper draught single screw steamers were preferred on the deep, choppier waters of the Hamoaze around Devonport Dockyard.

Coastal excursions were provided in the main by the liner tender fleet of the Great Western Railway at Millbay Docks. For nearly ninety years these tenders provided excursions to Salcombe, Looe, Fowey, Mevagissey, Falmouth and the Eddystone Lighthouse. Their regular job was ferrying liner passengers and mailbags from anchorages in Cawsand Bay and Plymouth Sound to Customs and the GWR's railway station at Millbay. Although these liner passengers were only aboard for one or two hours, the saloons and refreshment bars were comfortably fitted and the tenders were maintained to a high standard. Intruders like P&A Campbell Ltd's *Westward Ho*, Cosens & Co. Ltd's *Alexandra*, and Torbay Steamers Ltd's *Princess Elizabeth*, frantically splashing about looking for passengers, arrived in a blaze of publicity and after just two seasons quietly vanished. Plymouth's tenders, meanwhile, continued providing coastal excursions for the local population into the 1960s.

One
Exmouth district

'For children's gambols Oddicombe Beach would be difficult to excel for safety and convenience', so advised the Ward Lock Guide in 1899. Oddicombe, in Torquay, was also safe for the Devon Dock, Pier & Steamship Co. Ltd's paddle steamers to land because much shingle, originating from the adjacent Babbacombe Beach, had gathered there over the years, providing a good landing beach for the *Duchess of Devonshire*. She is seen *c*.1905, with a huge complement queuing to 'gambol' on the beach. The headland in the background is Petit Tor Point.

S.S. Duchess of Devonshire at Exmouth

The *Duchess of Devonshire* approaching Exmouth Pier in a postcard by John Land of Empire Stores, Exmouth. There is no beach landing gear in evidence, except the large searchlight on the bridge, forward of the funnel. This helped to light beach landing operations at dusk. The black umbrella is to keep the sun off – not rain. A familiar sight on the south Devon coast until 1934, the steel hulled *Duchess of Devonshire* was built in 1892 by R.&H. Green of London, with two-cylinder compound, diagonal engines by J. Penn & Sons of Greenwich.

An Art Co. of Seaton postcard, showing the *Duchess of Devonshire* at Seaton *c.*1905. Her paddle wheels can be seen turning slowly ahead to keep her on the beach. The fishing boats with masts are Beer luggers (the place not the drink), a distinctive type along the east facing coast of Lyme Bay. After the First World War they were gradually motorised and lost their mainsail.

The *Duchess of Devonshire* and (behind) the *Victoria* of Cosens & Co. Ltd of Weymouth, landing passengers on the beach at Seaton – from a postcard postmarked 1907. Judging from the bunting aboard and ashore, and the presence of a funfair, this was a special occasion. The two companies employed the same beach landing arrangement aboard their steamers. Before the First World War the *Victoria* sailed regularly to Torquay or Dartmouth from Bournemouth or Weymouth.

The Devon Dock, Pier & Steamship Co. Ltd's *Duchess of Devonshire* leaving Exmouth Pier in the 1920s. A nice touch for the helmsman is a protective canvas awning – quite cosy at a time when no protection at all was generally the order of the day on seasonal paddle steamers.

A phototyped or photogravured (i.e. printed without a dot screen) postcard, photographed by F.T. Blackburn of Budleigh Salterton, showing the *Duchess of Devonshire* at that beach in around 1910. Budleigh was a featured destination only when the *Duchess of Devonshire* started from Torquay, because it is literally just around the corner from Exmouth.

The Devon Dock, Pier & Steamship Co. Ltd's Exmouth Pier and *Duchess of Devonshire* in the 1920s. A significant post war alteration to the paddle steamer was the removal of her helm to a position forward of the funnel. She also lost her main mast (i.e. the one at the back).

Leaving Teignmouth.

The steel hulled *Duke of Devonshire* was built in 1896 by R.&H. Green. At 175ft, she was 5ft longer than her older fleet sister, but looked identical. In photographs the two paddlers are difficult to tell apart but the *Duke of Devonshire* had a slightly taller funnel and less paddle box vents. This similarity was used to the company's advantage on their own postcards, like this one, by scrubbing the steamer's name off the bows and selling them on both ships.

The *Duke of Devonshire* leaving a beach before the First World War, with the characteristic landing gear in the process of being stowed away.

Not south Devon, but West Bay, Bridport on the Dorset coast, a regular destination from Exmouth with a call at Lyme Regis. The *Duke of Devonshire* is pictured disembarking at the beach, soon after the First World War.

Two pictures taken aboard the *Duke of Devonshire* (the one numbered 223 in the 1920s and the other, 434, in the early thirties). The photographer was F.H. Wilson of Exmouth, who would have blown a whistle or shouted to get faces in the picture. His postcards were available for sale on the steamer's return, plainly, if crudely, numbered for extra prints. In the earlier picture note the crewman with a 'Duke of Devonshire' knitted jersey and, possibly, the Ladies Saloon stewardess standing in the companionway. In the later picture note the saloon skylight vents between the seats.

A Devon Dock, Pier & Steamship Co. Ltd official postcard of the *Duke of Devonshire* having just left Exmouth Pier. The card was posted on 6 August 1914 and an excerpt reads, 'Have just come from Dartmouth on this boat the 'Duke'. Went to Sidmouth yesterday'.

Laid up for the winter in Exmouth Docks are the Devon Dock, Pier & Steamship Co. Ltd's screw steamer *Prince Edward*, from their Torbay service; the *Duchess of Devonshire*; and the *Duke of Devonshire* (behind). The roof of the building on the quayside reads: 'D. D. P. & S. Co. ENGINEERS AND IRON WORKS'.

Exmouth Docks during the winter in the mid 1920s. Left to right: the *Starcross* from the Starcross Ferry; *Prince Edward* with a white hull; the *Melita* from the Starcross Ferry; the *Duchess of Devonshire* and the *Duke of Devonshire* (behind).

The *Duchess of Devonshire* was laid up as usual at the end of 1930 but never returned to service for the Devon Dock, Pier & Steamship Co. Ltd. She was sold in 1933 to the South Devon & West Bay Steamship Co. Ltd which operated her for one season out of Lyme Regis and in 1934 based her at Torquay. She is seen in that company's funnel colours at Sidmouth.

On Monday 27 August 1934 the *Duchess of Devonshire* made her final beach landing. The expression 'tempting fate' springs to mind when one recalls the hundreds of risky beach landings she and her old fleet mate, the *Duke of Devonshire*, had made over the years. It was an accident waiting to happen. Having dragged her kedge anchor, which held her at right angle to the beach, she swung around and grounded broadside on the beach. Unluckily she was holed by a concrete slab.

The *Duchess of Devonshire*'s passengers were landed safely but subsequent attempts at salvage failed and the forty-two-year-old ship was broken up on the beach.

The *Duke of Devonshire* was sold to Irish owners in 1934 and the Devon Dock, Pier & Steamship Co. Ltd withdrew from the coastal excursion business. After two years in Ireland she returned to south Devon in the ownership of Alexander Taylor, who ran her out of Torquay for two seasons. She is pictured during this period on a Seaward postcard approaching Weymouth. She was sold to Cosens & Co. Ltd of Weymouth in 1938 and renamed *Consul*.

The Starcross Ferry steamer *Prince* at Starcross. Note the railway wagons in the background on the GWR mainline. The *Prince* was built by Simpson & Strickland Co. Ltd of Dartmouth in 1891. She had a wooden hull and twin screws and was in service until the mid 1920s. This Chapman & Son of Dawlish postcard was posted in 1927.

The *Prince* is approaching Starcross Steps. This landing pier, extending from the original ferry steps, was built in 1846, more or less coinciding with the building of the South Devon Railway mainline from Exeter to Plymouth. The pier was lengthened by the GWR in 1904.

The wooden hulled *Melita* was built around 1895, possibly by Lavis of Exmouth. The helmsman can be seen in the bows. A consignment of parcels awaits collection at the top of the steps. *Melita* perpetuated the name of the very first steamer on the route, a converted barge in the 1880s.

The wooden hulled *Zulu* brought the Starcross Ferry fleet up to three. This single screw, wooden-hulled steamer was built *c.*1900 by Lavis of Exmouth and fitted with a triple expansion engine and a coal fired boiler. The ferry steps are inside the dock entrance at Exmouth. The postcard was photographed by R.E. Holden of Exmouth.

The Docks. Exmouth

Left: The *Prince* at Exmouth landing steps, with a trading ketch behind.

Below: Devon Dock Pier & Steamship Co. Ltd excursion ticket.

DEVON DOCK, PIER AND
STEAMSHIP CO., LTD.

RIVER EXE TRIP
(AFTERNOON)

NOT TRANSFERABLE AND AVAILABLE ONLY
ON THE DAY OF ISSUE.

Subject to conditions of the Company.

D66—Williamson, Ticket Printer, Ashton

2929

54984. EXMOUTH. STARCROSS FERRY.

The *Starcross*, on the left, was built of steel in Exmouth Docks by the Devon Dock, Pier & Steamship Co. Ltd in 1923. Her twin screws were powered by triple expansion engines by Sissons of Gloucester. She replaced the *Prince*, which can be seen on the right and therefore dates this picture *c*.1923. The middle steamer is the *Melita*.

The photographer F.H. Wilson, trading as Wilson's Snaps, of 7 Market Street, Exmouth, was active after the First World War. Passengers are pictured by him aboard the *Starcross* about to depart for an excursion, probably up river to Turf Locks – the entrance to Exeter Canal, or, tide permitting, to Topsham.

Passengers pictured aboard the *Starcross* at Exmouth in the mid 1920s. A group photograph by F.H. Wilson.

FERRY FROM STARCROSS.

The diesel age on the Starcross Ferry was heralded by the ex-Admiralty motor launch *Tamar Queen* (later just *Tamar*). Acquired in 1933 she was previously operated as a market day and excursion boat by the Tamar Transport Co. of Calstock. The forepeak offered shelter in bad weather. The little compartment in the stern is the engine room. The *Tamar Queen* replaced the steamer *Melita*.

The *Tamar* pictured in the 1950s at Exmouth ferry steps. She was withdrawn in 1954. This view also shows the swing bridge at the dock entrance.

Looks are not everything, it was the economy and efficiency of the diesel engined *Tamar* that attracted the Devon Dock, Pier & Steamship Co. Ltd. In 1934 they ordered a new boat from Lavis of Exmouth to replace the *Zulu*. Similar in appearance to the older steamers, she was diesel engined. So enamoured were the company with this motive power, they named her *Diesel Comet*. She is pictured at Exmouth in 1966 by Michael Messenger.

The *Orcombe* was built by Lavis in 1954 to replace the *Tamar*. She is pictured, with the *Diesel Comet* ahead, on the Exeter Canal. This rare event in 1968 was captured by a *Western Morning News* photographer.

One of many launches working along the south Devon coast with a local authority licence for twelve passengers – the maximum number before a Board of Trade certificate is required. This picture of the *Wilfred I* is by Vickery Bros of Exmouth, who specialised in group boat and char-a-banc pictures like this. The message on the back reads: 'Mum and Dad, taken at Exmouth, some photo, you must put your specks on to see me – taken July 28th. '24'.

The excursion boat *Devon Princess* at Exmouth in the 1960s. She was an ex-Royal Navy HDML (Harbour Defence Motor Launch) of 1945. Originally owned by Herbert Jennings, she was later operated by Devon Princess Cruises out of Exmouth and Torbay. From Exmouth she offered cruises to Sidmouth, Lyme Regis, Torquay, the River Dart, Brixham, into the River Teign, or up the Exe to Turf Locks or Topsham.

Something of a surprise on the River Exe, the paddle steamer *Sussex Queen* (ex-Southern Railway Solent ferry *Freshwater*) at Topsham in the winter of 1960-1961. She had operated as an excursion ship for one season at Brighton in 1960. For the following season she was again renamed – *Swanage Queen* – and ran between Bournemouth and Swanage. During these, her twighlight years, she was owned by Herbert Jennings of Budleigh Salterton – thus her lay up berth on the Exe.

Beach boats at Teignmouth during the halcyon years of the English beach resorts in the 1950s. A favourite excursion for these twelve seaters was around the pier and up the River Teign to Coombe Cellars, an attractive tea house on a promontory about two miles upriver.

The Teignmouth & Shaldon Bridge Co. were operators of the Shaldon Ferry when this picture was taken in the 1920s. The Shaldon Ferry boats have painted 'gun ports' around their hull. This distinctive device was perpetuated from the earlier rowboat ferries. The two ferry boats pictured here are probably No.1 and No.2, built at Dartmouth in 1907 and 1908 respectively. They were the first powered ferries on the service. Teignmouth is in the background.

Two
Tor Bay

The Plymouth registered *Plymouth Belle* appeared on the south Devon coast in 1895. She ran along the south Devon and Cornwall coast calling at Penzance, Falmouth, Mevagissey, Fowey, Plymouth and Torquay – where she is pictured. The Plymouth Belle Steamship Co. Ltd sought to keep her company 'select' (i.e. middle class) – her excursions were not cheap and weekend jaunts to the Channel Islands were three day affairs with hotel accommodation ashore. This probably signalled her downfall, it was difficult to fill her 1,350 capacity without hundreds of working class trippers to subsidise her operation – serves their right then. After just one season she was chartered to R.R. Collard of Newhaven to run excursions on the south coast of England and never returned to the south west.

Pictured from the end of Haldon Pier, the *Pride of Devon* has a good complement of passengers. Built in 1897 the *Pride of Devon* was originally named *Walton Belle* – one of the Belle Steamers fleet of the Thames coast. At the end of the Second World War (having been renamed *Essex Queen* by her second owners, the New Medway Steam Packet Co.) she was sold to the South Western Steam Navigation Co., which put her into service from Torquay in 1947.

HALDON PIER, TORQUAY.

Haldon Pier, Torquay c.1948 with the 522 tons gross paddle steamer *Pride of Devon* alongside. Unfortunately this expensive to run steamer was only offering very short 'trips around the bay' – no more than a diesel boat, a fraction of her size, could offer. After two seasons the ancient steamer finally gave up the ghost and failed her Board of Trade inspection. She was laid up at Southampton and scrapped on the Thames in 1951.

In 1950 the turbine steamer *Lady Enchantress* arrived in Torquay for what E.C.B. Thornton, in his book *South Coast Pleasure Steamers*, kindly called an experiment. Bought by the Three Star Shipping Co. from the Admiralty in 1946 she was tried unsuccessfully on the Thames coast and in 1950 came, inevitably, to Torquay. She lasted less than a month when she became disabled near the Casquets rocks on a Channel Islands trip. This picture shows her being towed back to Torquay (and oblivion) by the tug *Turmoil*. Note the tow rope and her black 'not under control' ball on her foremast.

The parade of Torquay's 'coffin dodging' excursion steamers continued and P&A Campbell Ltd's *Empress Queen* was next to try her luck. She is moored at Haldon Pier in 1951. She offered excursions as far a Bournemouth, Falmouth and across the channel to Guernsey but after only one season she returned Bristol and was laid-up, never to run in British waters again. Ahead lies the diesel engined *Kiloran* of the Devon Cruising Co. Ltd, seemingly a far more suitable vessel for the Torquay trade.

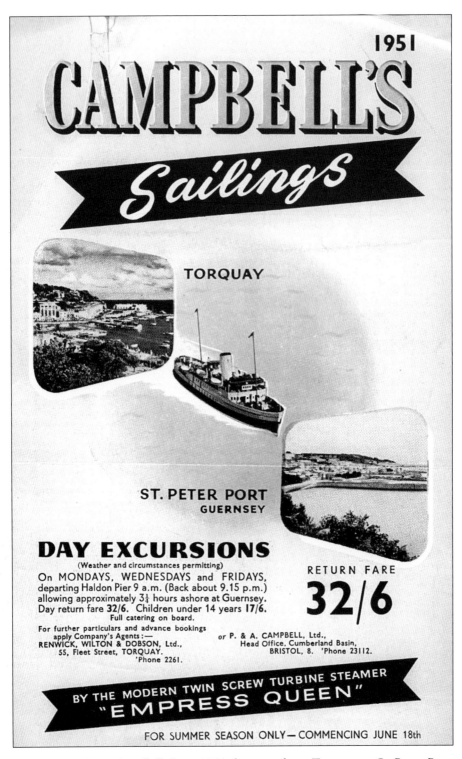

An *Empress Queen* handbill from 1951 for trips from Torquay to St Peter Port, Guernsey – with around three hours ashore.

Haldon Pier c.1960. The big steamer on the right is yet another itinerant, the *St Patrick* of the British Transport Commission, looking for work after redundancy at Weymouth. She ran occasionally from Torquay to the Channel Islands until she was transferred to Dover in the mid 1960s. On the left is the ex-Royal Navy Fairmile B launch *Kiloran II* which replaced her earlier namesake and offered trips in Tor Bay and on the River Dart.

From left to right: the *St Patrick* (behind) at Haldon Pier; the *Regency Belle*, Torquay's own excursion vessel, at Princess Pier; and, on the right, the quaint looking Solent ferry paddler *Princess Elizabeth* – another hopeful looking for work. The latter named steamer was operated by Torbay Steamers Ltd from 1960, running mostly to Lyme Regis, Dartmouth and Plymouth. This time even Torquay Borough Council conspired in her demise and, after *Princess Elizabeth*'s skipper had a falling-out with Torquay's Harbourmaster, they effectively cut off the old paddlers' oil supply – farewell *Princess Elizabeth*.

The *Waverley*, pictured by C.H.S. Owen at Haldon Pier on 29 May 1979, continuing the long tradition of brief visits by coastal steamers.

TORBAY SEAWAYS - *for the Channel Islands*

Redundant passenger ships were still beating a path to Torquay in 1982. The ex-Isles of Scilly ferry *Scillonian II* was renamed *Devonia* by P&A Campbell Ltd to operate (unsuccessfully) in the Bristol Channel. Torbay Seaways bought her in 1982 to maintain a service between Torquay and the Channel Islands. She was renamed *Devoniun* because the moribund Bristol company wanted to keep the name. This commemorative postcard for the *Devoniun's* maiden crossing to Guernsey was posted aboard the ship.

34

Pictured by Paul Clegg the *Devoniun* is docked at St Peter Port, Guernsey in 1982.

In an attempt to improve upon the crane loading of cars, the *Devoniun* was sold in 1984 and the ex-Caledonian MacBrayne's *Clansman* was purchased for her stern loading capability. But Torbay District Council were opposed to a linkspan in the harbour and the *Clansman* was sold without being used. The passenger only hydrofoil *Star Capricorn* was tried in 1985 with disappointing results. In 1986 Torbay Seaways bought the 1,420 tons gross ex-Caledonian MacBrayne *Hebrides*, with a side loading facility for vehicles, and arrived at an operating agreement with the council. Renamed *Devoniun* she successfully maintained services from Torquay to the Channel Islands until Torbay Seaways Ltd was taken over by Jersey based Huelin Renouf Shipping in 1990. The new owners closed the passenger service at the end of the year. The second *Devoniun* is pictured in the Channel Islands in the late 1980s

Souvenir

Photograph

TAKEN ABOARD THE

REGENCY BELLE

TORQUAY

It's sad that a souvenir photograph like this ended up in a printed ephemera box at an antique fair – did nobody have happy memories of either the holiday or the girls? The picture and souvenir folder are evocative of endless summers of the fifties and sixties, when the English beach resort was in its prime and Torquay at last enjoyed some suitable excursion services. The photographer, W. Moxley, would have your souvenir prints ready when the boat returned.

The 251 tons gross, 128ft long *Regency Belle* was built in New York Harbour in 1942 as a motor minesweeper and was transferred to the Royal Navy as HMS *Radcliffe* under the Lend-Lease Agreement. After the Second World War she was converted as a passenger boat and worked at Brighton (thus '*Regency*' *Belle*) and Scarborough before arriving at Torquay in 1955. Operated by the Torquay Cruising Co. Ltd, the *Regency Belle* stayed in Torquay until 1963, when the Western Lady Ferry Service Ltd gained control of Torquay Cruising Co. Ltd and sold the *Regency Belle* as an oil rig tender.

The Devon Cruising Co. Ltd's *Kiloran* was based at Torquay during the 1950s, and was seemingly an ideal vessel for operations from the south Devon harbour. The message from this postcard reads: 'Having our first boat trip today, up the river Dart to Dittisham, on the boat shown on this card.'

In 1957 the *Kiloran* was replaced by the ex-Royal Navy Fairmile B motor launch (ML) *Kiloran II*. She was built in 1941 by J. Sadd of Maldon and was 112ft long. Converted for passenger work she ran for a while from Conway as the *Cambrian Prince*. At Torquay she undertook cruises to the River Dart. In November 1963 she was sold to the Cornish Sea Cruising Co. and worked out of St Mawes in Cornwall.

The South Western Steam Navigation Co. Ltd's *Pride of the Bay* was formerly the *Leven* of the Caledonian Steam Packet Co. Ltd. She was built in 1938 by Wm Denny & Bros Ltd and measured 38 tons gross, 60ft long x 13.5ft wide x 5.1ft deep. She was purchased by the South Western Steam Navigation Co. Ltd of Paignton in 1965.

The *Torbay Prince* was unique – being the only vessel purpose built to run excursions from Torquay. She was built by M.W. Blackmore & Sons of Bideford in 1947 for the Devon Star Shipping Co. Ltd (J. Kerr). For many years she ran trips to Babbacombe Bay, the River Dart and around Tor Bay, from Princess Pier. She had a wooden hull and measured 91 tons gross, 81ft long and 19ft wide. This picture was the *Torbay Prince*'s official postcard.

The *Torbay Prince* in Tor Bay in the 1950s. She was sold in 1967 and endured a nomadic career around the British Isles, during which time she acquired the name *Tudor Prince*. She was rescued from virtual dereliction by George Pill's Cornish Ferry (Red Funnel) Co. Ltd of Falmouth in 1981. Currently over fifty years old she is still running on the River Fal.

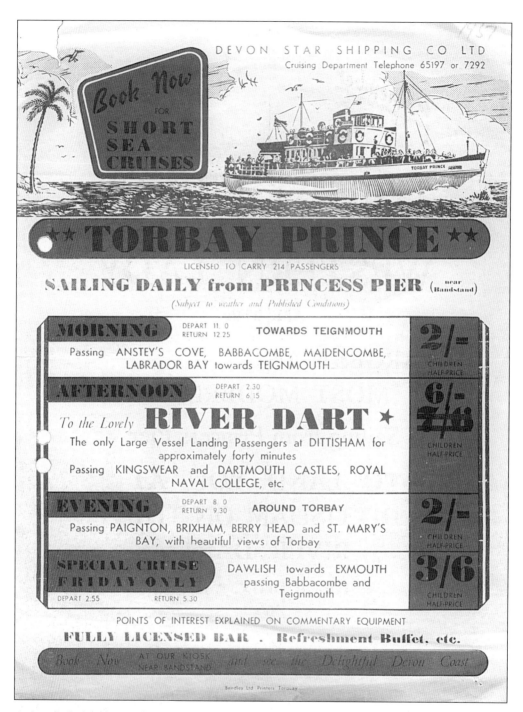

A handbill for the *Torbay Prince*, dating from 1957. Her trips to the Dart were run in conjunction with the *Western Lady* of the Western Lady Ferry Services Ltd.

Never having quite understood the holiday maker's fascination for Torquay, I can, conversely, fully appreciate the popularity of a ferry service out of Torquay and across Tor Bay to the fishing harbour of Brixham. Pictured at Princess Gardens Jetty (since demolished) is the steamboat *Pioneer*, one of the first to run the Tor Bay steamer service from Torquay, calling at Paignton and Brixham. The funnel on the far side of the jetty belongs to the Devon Dock, Pier & Steamship Co. Ltd's steamer, *King Edward* – the *Pioneer*'s opposition on the route.

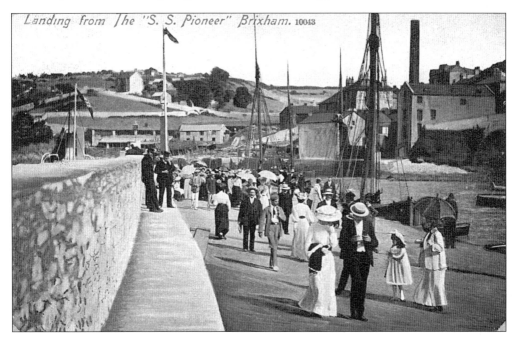

A postcard by Currie & Cliffe of Teignmouth shows passengers arriving on Brixham's New Pier, having disembarked from the *Pioneer*, the funnel and name pennant of which can be seen behind the quay wall.

The Devon Dock, Pier & Steamship Co. Ltd's *King Edward* arriving at New Pier, Brixham. The steamers always berthed on the outside of the pier. In the background some of Brixham's trawler fleet can be seen leaving the harbour. The twin screw steamer *King Edward* was built by Philips of Dartmouth in 1901 and measured 52 tons gross and 70ft long.

BOAT PIER & BERRY HEAD, BRIXHAM. (507)

In 1902 the Devon Dock, Pier & Steamship Co. Ltd bought the 61 tons gross, twin screw, passenger tug *Lord Kitchener* from Southampton to support the *Prince Edward*. In 1921 the *Lord Kitchener* was renamed *Countess of Devon* and registered in Exeter. It is in this guise that she is seen alongside New Pier in 1922. She was sold in 1926.

The *King Edward* approaching the landing stage on New Pier, Brixham. Note the wagonettes inside the quay wall, waiting for passengers from the steamer. By 1930 the Devon Dock, Pier & Steamship Co. Ltd had stopped running the Tor Bay ferry and the *Prince Edward* was sold.

M.V. "WESTERN LADY. TORQUAY & BRIXHAM

After the Second World War, in 1947, the Tor Bay ferry service was revived by Ronald Edhouse and his son, initially using three ex-Royal Navy Fairmile B motor launches, bought without engines. The vessels were all named *Western Lady* – with suffix numbers – and sailed from Princess Pier, Torquay to New Pier, Brixham. *Western Lady* is pictured approaching Torquay on this official 'postcard', which has a Western Lady publicity message on the back.

Two Western Lady Fairmile launches at Brixham New Pier in 1951. A profusion of bunting and a healthy complement of passengers indicates a special occasion. The *Western Lady*, approaching the pier on the left, was built for the Royal Navy as RML 535 in 1941, by W. Wetherhead & Son of Cockenzie (near Edinburgh). During the Second World War she was stationed at Plymouth.

Western Lady II, ex RML 542, was built in 1942 by Austins of East Ham (Furniture Manufacturers). She was sold in 1955 and converted for private use.

Western Lady V – not a Fairmile launch but ex-*Southend Britannia*, 147 tons gross, 115ft long and built by Thornycroft's in 1924. She was purchased to replace *Western Lady II* in 1956 but was sold back to the Thames four years later – for a static role.

WESTERN LADY FERRY SERVICE, LTD.

THE QUAY, BRIXHAM.

Phone: Brixham 2041
Torquay 7292

(Proprietors: R. E. EDHOUSE & SON)

A Ferry Service and Pleasure Cruise combined.

Torquay to Brixham

and vice versa.

THESE MOTOR SHIPS

WESTERN LADY	WESTERN LADY III
WESTERN LADY II	WESTERN LADY IV

are the LARGEST, Fastest
and most modern Ships

Sailing from The PRINCESS PIER, TORQUAY
and The QUAY, BRIXHAM.

enabling you to view the beautiful coastline of Torbay.

BRIXHAM (Dept. Pier)	TORQUAY (Arr. Princess Pier)	TORQUAY (Dept. Princess Pier)	BRIXHAM (Arr. Pier)
9-00 a.m.	9-30 a.m.	9-45 a.m.	10-15 a.m.
9-45	10-15	10-30	11-00
10-30	11-00	11-15	11-45
11-15	11-45	12-00 noon	12-30 p.m.
12-00 noon	12-30 p.m.	12-45 p.m.	1-15
12-45 p.m.	1-15	2-15	2-45
2-15	2-45	3-00	3-30
3-00	3-30	3-45	4-15
3-45	4-15	4-30	5-00
4-30	5-00	5-15	5-45
5-15	5-45	6-00	6-30
6-00	6-30	6-45	7.15
6-45	7-15	7-30	8-00
7-30	8-00	8-00	8-30
8-45	9-15	9-30	10-00

Commencing at 9-0 a.m. Weather and other circumstances permitting.

FARE — 1/- Return (including Toll at Brixham) 6d. Single

CHILDREN UNDER 12 HALF PRICE.

Return Fare Passengers may disembark and return by a later Sailing. Pay Office at entrance to each Pier

CIRCULAR TOUR By ROAD & SEA AROUND TORBAY

by any Western Lady Ship or Devon General Bus on the Brixham to Torquay Service, and vice versa

FARE 1/9 RETURN CHILDREN 1/3

Pay Office at entrance to each Pier and Devon General Booking Offices

All Ships are fitted with Up-to-Date and Spacious Deck Saloons affording maximum comfort and observation in any weather.

Goad, Printer, Brixham.

Western Lady Ferry Service Ltd timetable from 1951.

Western Lady IV, ex *RML 526*, was built by the Solent Shipyard in 1942. She joined the Western Lady fleet in 1949 after being purchased at an auction in Fowey. *Western Lady IV* is one of two surviving Fairmile B launches still running the Western Lady Ferry Service – the other being *Western Lady III*.

The Western Lady Ferry Service Ltd fleet in the late 1950s (with twin funnelled *Western Lady V* on the far left), anchored in Brixham's Outer Harbour.

Western Lady Ferry Service Ltd timetable cover from 2000, with the *Western Lady III* featured. *Western Lady III*, ex RML 497, was built in 1941 by the Southampton Steam Joinery Co. Ltd.

A Chapman & Son postcard from the 1920s (the card is dated on the reverse: June 7th 1929). An unidentified motor launch is pictured at Anstey's Cove, Torquay. The plaque on the mast offers: 'Trips in the Bay'. Note how well covered everybody is.

More 'twelves' – i.e. boats licenced by the local authority for a maximum of twelve passengers, in Babbacombe Bay during 1931. The sunseekers are still fairly well wrapped up.

Three
River Dart

The *Berry Castle* of 1880 at Steamer Quay, Totnes. She was an iron steamer, built at Polybank's yard in Kingswear and fitted out by Alexander Philip at Sandquay Yard (before his move to Noss Works, across the river). She measured 73.3 tons gross, 108ft long x 14.1ft wide x 5.1ft deep and had two cylinder oscillating engines (built in London). She was the prototype upon which all future River Dart Steamboat Co. Ltd paddle steamers would be based, culminating with the *Kingswear Castle* of 1924, which is still operational, albeit on the River Medway in Kent. In this picture the *Berry Castle* is wearing the black funnel colour and pennant of the Dartmouth & Torbay Steam Packet Co.

The *Berry Castle* steaming down Home Reach on the River Dart, with Totnes in the background. Just behind the *Berry Castle* is the *Kingswear Castle* of 1904 approaching Steamer Quay. In 1906 the River Dart Steamboat Co. Ltd was incorporated and took over the Dartmouth & Torbay Steam Packet Co.'s four paddle steamers: *Berry Castle, Dartmouth Castle, Totnes Castle* and *Kingswear Castle*. It is the yellow and black funnel colours of the River Dart Steamboat Co. Ltd that the *Berry Castle* is wearing in this *c.*1910 photograph.

The *Dartmouth Castle* at Steamer Quay, Totnes *c*.1910. This steel paddle steamer was built in 1885 by Harvey & Co. Ltd of Hayle and measured 59.4 tons gross, 100ft long x 13ft wide x 6.3ft deep.

The steel hulled *Kingswear Castle* of 1904 at Steamer Quay. She was built by Cox & Co. of Falmouth and measured 85 tons gross, 107.6ft long x 15.1ft wide x 5ft deep. Cox & Co. also built her two cylinder compound diagonal engines. These engines survive in the Paddle Steamer Preservation Society's *Kingswear Castle* – having been transferred to the latter steamer when she was built in 1924.

The *Kingswear Castle* of 1904 approaching Steamer Quay, Totnes.

The hulked *Kingswear Castle* of 1904 forming part of the river bank at Fleet Mill Quay, just downstream from Home Reach on the River Dart. Her remains can still be seen today.

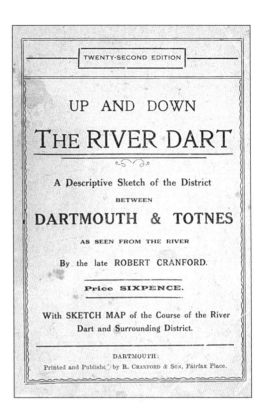

'Up and down the Dart' was the motto emblazoned on the paddle boxes of the Dart paddlers. The phrase was taken from Robert Cranford's little guide book, which was the official guide sold aboard the steamers until the Second World War.

The *Compton Castle* of 1914 heading down the River Dart near Totnes in the 1950s. She was built by Cox & Co. of Falmouth and measured 71 tons gross, 100.4ft long x 14.6ft wide x 5.3ft deep. Cox also built her two cylinder compound diagonal engines. The *Compton Castle* was the first of Dart paddlers to have her passenger deck extended over her paddle sponsons and to have portholes, replacing the rectangular windows of the earlier steamers.

The *Compton Castle* at Steamer Quay, Totnes in the 1950s.

The *Totnes Castle* of 1923 embarking passengers at Totnes in 1925. She was built by Philip & Son Ltd of Dartmouth and measured 94 tons gross, 108ft long x 17.6ft wide x 3ft deep, with two cylinder compound diagonal engines.

The *Totnes Castle* (outside) and the *Kingswear Castle* of 1924, pictured at Totnes in the 1930s. The *Kingswear Castle* was built by Philip & Son Ltd. She was the same size as the *Totnes Castle* but her gross tonnage was calculated as 94 as opposed to the former's 91. Both steamers carried 400 passengers. The *Kingswear Castle* was fitted with her earlier namesake's Cox & Co. engines.

The *Kingswear Castle* of 1924, pictured in the 1930s, approaching the South Embankment in Dartmouth Harbour.

The *Kingswear Castle* steaming down Home Reach, below Totnes.

Photographed by the River Dart Steamboat Co. Ltd's Manager, L.H. Hobbs in 1947, for use on leaflets and handbills. The two steamers are *Totnes Castle* (nearest) and *Kingswear Castle*, in Dartmouth Harbour.

UP AND DOWN

THE RIVER DART

SOUVENIR OF THE TRIP . ONE SHILLING

Another Hobbs picture, used on the company's souvenir handbook – an updated version of Robert Cranford's *Up and down the River Dart*.

TS8 RIVER DART STEAMER AT TOTNES

The *Totnes Castle* turning at Totnes in the early 1960s and demonstrating the reason for the maximum 108ft length of these steamers. She was withdrawn in 1963 and sold for static use in Dartmouth Harbour in the following year.

Pictured by Bernard Cox on 9 July 1965, the ex-River Dart Steamboat Co. Ltd paddle steamer *Totnes Castle* serves as an accommodation vessel for a floating hostel/sailing school in Dartmouth Harbour. She was sold for breaking in 1967 but sank under tow, in Bigbury Bay.

The *Kingswear Castle* and the *Compton Castle* at Steamer Quay in the 1960s. The *Compton Castle* was withdrawn in 1962-1963 and sold for static use at Kingsbridge in 1964.

Above: The *Kingswear Castle* pictured by Bernard Cox on 7 July 1965 at Steamer Quay, Totnes. Two months later she was withdrawn from service. Following two years of agonising, the Paddle Steamer Preservation Society bought the paddler for £600 – a special deal brokered by the River Dart Steamboat Co. Ltd Manager, L.H. Hobbs, because of 'sentiment and the fact that the old vessel was the last of the line'.

Right: A fundraising handbill by the Paddle Steamer Preservation Society.

The Paddle Steamer Preservation Society

Can We Interest You in a Paddle Steamer?

The paddle steamer concerned is the KINGSWEAR CASTLE—the smaller of our two paddle steamers. P. A. Vicary's photo below shows her at work in the 1950s, loaded with a happy holiday throng!

P.S. *Kingswear Castle*   P. A. Vicary

KINGSWEAR CASTLE is currently out of service. Our larger sea-going steamer WAVERLEY operates each Summer on the Clyde, with visits south in the Spring. She brings pleasure to thousands – *We are proud of our success with WAVERLEY – We are impatient for KINGSWEAR CASTLE to join her in exciting and useful service.*

With a gross tonnage of 94 KINGSWEAR CASTLE is quite a bit smaller than WAVERLEY, but is a most attractive coal fired river steamer. Built in 1924 by Philip & Son of Dartmouth, with a 2-cylinder compound diagonal engines of 1904 vintage transferred from an earlier paddler, she is typical of the small steamers that once served the public

R·D·S

SOUVENIR
BROCHURE

(with Postcards)

★

ONE
SHILLING

The internal combustion age of the River Dart Steamboat Co. Ltd began back in 1921 with the paraffin engined *Berry Castle*. The *Conway Castle*, pictured on the cover of this souvenir brochure, was the company's ninth motor vessel, built in 1963 by Philip & Son Ltd. Her wheelhouse was rescued from the paddle steamer *Compton Castle*. Her Welsh name reflects new ownership of the River Dart Steamboat Co. Ltd by Evans & Reid Investment Co. Ltd of Cardiff – this insensitive nomenclature was continued with the company's next new boat, the *Cardiff Castle*.

G.H. Ridalls & Sons included the *Dartmothian* in their ever changing fleet of red hulled motor vessels. She was built by Messrs Ferris and Bank of Dartmouth in 1938 as the *Seymour Castle* for the River Dart Steamboat Co. Ltd. She is pictured in the 1980s in the Long Stream on the River Dart.

The *Cardiff Castle* at Totnes in 1986. She was the last boat built for the River Dart Steamboat Co. Ltd in 1964. After a period of ownership by the Millbrook Steamboat & Trading Co. Ltd, on the River Tamar, during which time her appearance was greatly enhanced by construction of a deckhouse and a new wheelhouse, the *Cardiff Castle* returned to the Dart in the ownership of Dart Pleasure Craft Ltd.

A postcard by messrs Balley and Flower of Dartmouth showing the *Duchess of Devonshire* entering Dartmouth Harbour, pictured from Dartmouth Castle at the river mouth.

The *Duchess of Devonshire* moored off Dartmouth and landing passengers by local boats. At high tide steamers like the Exmouth paddlers could moor alongside the South Embankment.

The *Duke of Devonshire* was sold to P&A Campbell Ltd in 1933. After one season laid up at Exmouth Campbells sold her to Irish owners. She returned to south Devon in 1936 but was sold to Cosens & Co. Ltd of Weymouth in 1938. Renamed the *Consul* she enjoyed a long and successful new career on the Wessex coast. Sold for static use at Dartmouth in 1964, she was renamed the *Duke of Devonshire*. She is pictured in Dartmouth Harbour during this period. In 1968 she was towed to Southampton and scrapped.

Cosens & Co. Ltd's paddle steamer *Alexandra* was an earlier 'carpet-bagger' in south Devon. She was sent looking for employment in 1925, based at Torquay and running to Lyme Regis and Plymouth. She is pictured off Kingswear on a postcard by E. Wise of the Dart Developing Service of Dartmouth. The 'C' on her funnel was to help distinguish her from the similar Devon Dock Pier & Steamship Co. Ltd paddlers. There are not many passengers aboard. Her incursion lasted until 1927 when the Exmouth company paid Cosens & Co. Ltd to go away.

The *Princess Elizabeth*, with few passengers aboard, entering Dartmouth Harbour in 1960 or 1961. Considering that the previous picture of the *Alexandra* was taken in the mid 1920s, the similar looking *Princess Elizabeth* must have appeared like a museum piece on the eve of the swinging-sixties.

The ill fated *Lady Enchantress*, moored upstream of Philip & Sons Ltd shipyard on the Dart. This was possibly subsequent to her disastrous breakdown in the Channel Islands in 1950.

The *Regency Belle* in Dartmouth Harbour, looking every inch the product of an American shipyard. Some steamer historians seem to have a mental block where motor vessels are concerned. While paddle steamers like the *Duchess of Devonshire* are accepted as fully fledged ships or coastal cruising vessels, the *Regency Belle* is condescendingly categorised as a small motor vessel, even though she was bigger than the Exmouth paddler.

The South Western Steam Navigation Co. Ltd's *Pride of Paignton* was an ex-Royal Navy Fairmile B motor launch, built in 1942. She worked out of Paignton and Torquay running trips in Tor Bay and to the River Dart.

The *Beach Belle* pictured on the Dart passing laid-up shipping below Greenway. She was built by M.W. Blackmore & Sons of Bideford in 1926 as the 40 tons gross, twin screw *Worcester Castle* and worked originally out of Aberystwyth. Sold *c*.1950 as a candidate for conversion to a houseboat, she was virtually abandoned but rescued by George Newman of Tolverne Cottage on the River Fal and re-entered passenger service as the *Skylark of Tolverne*. In 1962 she was sold to Colin Bewley of Paignton and operated for two seasons on the Dart as the *Beach Belle*.

Dartmouth Lower Ferry runs from a slipway in Bayards Cove, Dartmouth to a slipway in Kingswear, adjacent to the Kingswear Railway Ferry. This small vehicular ferry is worked by tugs propelling pontoons. In this picture the steam pinnace *Forester* – the earliest powered boat on the ferry – is manouvering to turn, by pivoting her bow against the pontoon, and head for Kingswear in the background – the ferry slip is on the extreme right.

29. The Dart is crossed to Dartmouth.

The Lower Ferry in the 1950s, with one of the later diesel tugs, each named *Hauley* with numerical suffixes. Although seemingly descriptive of the work they perform, the *Hauley* tugs are named after a local historical worthy.

One of three ferry boats introduced by Dartmouth Council between the two world wars, to supplement the Lower Ferry vehicle pontoons. Named the *Reliance*, *Perseverance* and *Newcomin*, they ran between Dartmouth's South Embankment and Kingswear slipway. In the background *The Mew* has just left Kingswear pontoon.

DARTMOUTH.—FROM KINGSWEAR PIER

The Railway Ferry in Dartmouth Harbour runs from Kingswear's railway station pontoon to the pontoon on the Dartmouth side. The café on South Embankment that looks a bit like a station building was indeed formerly Dartmouth's railway station – 'the station without trains' – and the pontoon that survived until the 1980s was accessed through the station. In this postcard the paddle steamer *Dolphin* lies alongside Kingswear pontoon. The card is postmarked 1905, the *Dolphin*, therefore, had been part of the Great Western Railway fleet for three years, the ferry having previously been leased to the Dartmouth Steam Packet Co. Ltd.

The *Dolphin* off Kingswear *c.*1905 with the GWR's pontoon landing on the left. The *Dolphin* was built in 1869 by Harvey & Co. Ltd of Hayle. She was double ended and could leave the pontoons quite happily in either direction. She measured 61 tons gross, 104.6ft long x 15.2ft wide x 6.4ft deep.

The deck house of the *Dolphin* offered shelter on wet or stormy crossings. However, the rabble were excluded on 7 March 1902 when the deckhouse was fitted out for the royal crossing of King Edward VII and Queen Alexandra for the opening of the Royal Naval College, HMS *Britannia*. In the event nobody even saw the saloon because the King stood on the bridge and the rest of the royal party stayed on deck. The *Dolphin* was sold for scrap in 1908.

The *Dolphin's* replacement was the long lasting and well remembered *The Mew*, built by Cox & Co. of Falmouth in 1908. She was a steel screw steamer measuring 117 tons gross, 90.2ft long x 22.4ft wide x 8.3ft deep. She is pictured approaching Kingswear, as built, with her saloons extending into the stern section. Note the Royal Naval College, HMS *Britannia*, in the background.

A postcard by E.J. Wise of the Dart Developing Service shows *The Mew* approaching Dartmouth pontoon. After the First World War her after saloon was demolished and the deck strengthened to carry road vehicles, mainly the GWR's own delivery lorries. To reach the quayside the vehicles had to be driven up the pontoon bridges. A private car can be seen on the after deck in this view.

The Dartmouth pontoon with the station building behind and *The Mew* approaching.

The Mew's new squatter funnel was installed, along with other alterations, when she passed to British Railways in the Nationalisation of the railways in 1948. She is pictured during her last year in service – her final crossing was on 8 October 1954, witnessed by crowds ashore and saluted by rockets, boats whistles and sirens.

Paddle steamers of the River Dart Steamboat Co. Ltd were chartered to run on the railway ferry when *The Mew* was out of service for maintenance and after she was withdrawn. The *Kingswear Castle* is pictured on the ferry in the 1950s. This useful employment dried up when British Railways initially chartered the *Lady Elizabeth*, a Plymouth district motor launch and later took delivery of two purpose built motor boats for use on the ferry.

The *Adrian Gilbert* and *Humphrey Gilbert* were built in 1957 by M.W. Blackmore & Sons of Bideford for the British Railways railway ferry at Kingswear. The *Humphrey Gilbert* is pictured on delivery at Kingswear.

The *Adrian Gilbert* pictured at Dartmouth pontoon in the early 1980s. Following a nomadic existence after British Rail abandoned the line to Kingsbridge in 1972, the *Adrian Gilbert* returned to Dartmouth in 1977 and the *Humphrey Gilbert* (renamed the *Edgcumbe Belle*) in 1985, both in the ownership of Dart Pleasure Craft Ltd. The *Adrian Gilbert* has since gone to the River Fal.

The Higher Ferry, upstream of Dartmouth, is a floating bridge. This picture shows the ex-Saltash floating bridge (of 1865) at Dartmouth c.1892. She seems to have been tried out on the ferry service but was replaced by a Philip & Son Ltd built floating bridge in 1896.

In 1920 Philip & Son Ltd took over the ferry operation and installed a new floating bridge. The new vessel discarded the previous method of being propelled along chains and was, instead, driven by paddle wheels and guided by wires. This floating bridge is pictured in this E. Wise postcard with the ferry slip and GWR train in the background, on the Noss shore.

The Higher Ferry floating bridge in the 1950s. Note the wire guides and paddle wheel – she was, by definition, a paddle steamer.

Greenway from Dittisham.   E 31559

The Greenway Ferry runs between Greenway Quay, seen in the background, and Dittisham. This postcard shows the horseboat, which was propelled with long sweeps or oars. Later a motor boat was used as a tug, similar to the Lower Ferry in Dartmouth Harbour. The ferry is currently for passengers only and is worked by a small motor boat.

Four
Kingsbridge Estuary and District

The paddle steamer *Express*, pictured at New Quay, Kingsbridge. She was a coastal passenger/cargo packet which worked between Kingsbridge, Salcombe and Plymouth's Sutton Harbour. The *Express* was built by William Date of Kingsbridge in 1885. She was sold as an excursion steamer to Plymouth in 1893 and converted to a three masted schooner by 1900. The *Express* was sunk by a U-Boat in 1915.

The *Kingsbridge Packet* ran in opposition to the *Express*, on the same route. This iron screw steamer was built in 1879 by Harvey & Co. Ltd of Hayle and measured 110 tons gross, 102ft long x 19.5ft wide x 9ft deep. She is pictured in Salcombe Harbour by Dartmouth photographers Balley and Flower.

A replacement for the *Kingsbridge Packet* was the *Kingsbridge Packet* of 1908, built by Cox & Co. of Falmouth. She measured 128 tons gross, 103.2ft long x 19.7ft wide x 9.2ft deep. After the First World War, with passenger traffic increasingly hard to generate, the *Kingsbridge Packet* discontinued her passenger service and was sent coasting as a cargo steamer.

A postcard by A.E. Fairweather of Salcombe showing the *Kingsbridge Packet* (of 1908) steaming up the Kingsbridge Estuary. Note: the local sailing barge – competition to the *Kingsbridge Packet*; the houseboat – ex-Kingsbridge Estuary paddle steamer *Reindeer*; and Kingsbridge at the top of the estuary.

Salcombe Harbour in 1896. Entering the harbour is the GWR liner tender *Sir Francis Drake* on an excursion from Plymouth. Anchored on the right is the, then new, *Duke of Devonshire* from Exmouth or Torquay disembarking passengers by local boats. For the eagle eyed, behind the foremast of the Exmouth paddler is the Kingsbridge Estuary paddle steamer *Reindeer*.

The *Sir Francis Drake* in Salcombe Harbour c.1910.

The *Channel Queen* moored in Salcombe Harbour, off the Portlemouth side, disembarking passengers on an excursion from Plymouth. The *Channel Queen* was built in Middlesborough in 1895 for the Plymouth, Channel Islands & Brittany Steamship Co. and maintained services indicated by the company name. She also ran excursions along the south Devon and Cornwall coast to Salcombe, Looe, Polperro and Fowey. Her short career ended in 1898 when she was wrecked in the Channel Islands with the loss of ten lives.

The GWR liner tender, *Sir Richard Grenville*, at Salcombe just after the Second World War – a regular excursion destination for the tenders from Plymouth. The *Sir Richard Grenville* was the last steamer built for ocean liner tendering at Plymouth and was finally withdrawn from service in October 1963, when Plymouth's Millbay Docks closed as a mail port.

The general appearance of the Kingsbridge Estuary paddler *Reindeer* suggests that her builder had never actually seen a paddle steamer, but was working from a third party description. I am sure this is not the case as her builder, William Date of Kingsbridge, produced many fine schooners and brigantines but suffice to say, the *Reindeer* was not his finest hour. For twenty years or more she maintained Salcombe's link with Kingsbridge, at the top of the estuary.

The *Reindeer* at South Sands, where passengers were landed to walk around to Bolt Head. She was built in 1875 and measured 44.5 tons gross and 71ft long. Although her registry was not closed until 1906, she had been lying out of use for some years before. She was then converted as a houseboat moored on the Portlemouth side of the estuary. Finally abandoned the *Reindeer* rotted away in the estuary.

The *Salcombe Castle*, pictured approaching Kingsbridge c.1900. She effectively replaced the *Reindeer*, although ownership was different. She was built by Philip & Son Ltd in 1898 and measured 34 tons gross, 61.5ft long x 12ft wide x 6.75ft deep. The steamer service became busier once the railway arrived at Kingsbridge in 1893, especially after the hoped for extension to Salcombe failed to materialise. Indeed, until motor road transport made its appearance after the First World War, the estuary's steamers provided the most efficient link between Kingsbridge and Salcombe.

The *Salcombe Castle* moored at Kingsbridge.

Such was the growth in passenger traffic that in 1906, Nicholas March, owner of the *Salcombe Castle*, took delivery of a second steel paddler from Willoughby Bros Ltd of Stonehouse (now part of Plymouth). Named *Ilton Castle* she measured 52.5 tons gross, 80.5ft long x 13.5ft wide x 4.8ft deep and was fitted with compound diagonal engines, also by Willoughbys. The *Ilton Castle* is pictured prior to her maiden trip from Salcombe on 21 February 1906.

The *Ilton Castle* moored off Customs House Quay – the steamer landing in Salcombe. The trading smack is the barge *Yealm* from Plymouth, a regular caller.

ILTON CASTLE, SALCOMBE. No.198

An A.E. Fairweather postcard of the *Ilton Castle* steaming upstream, complete with a brass band. In the distance, behind her stern, is the *Reindeer*, converted to a houseboat.

Nicholas Southwood inherited the Kingsbridge Estuary paddlers in 1912. He returned to the shipyard of Willoughby & Sons Ltd in 1914 for a third paddle steamer, the *Kenwith Castle* – similar in appearance and dimensions to the *Ilton Castle*. It is unclear whether the new steamer was intended as a replacement for the *Salcombe Castle*, or as a third steamer. The First World War undoubtedly ruined Nicholas Southwood's plans and the *Salcombe Castle*, although only sixteen years old, was laid up, never to be used again. This A.E. Fairweather postcard shows the *Kenwith Castle* in Salcombe Harbour with a 'complimentary trip' – which, judging from the number of children aboard, was a free trip for them.

The *Kenwith Castle* approaching New Quay, Kingsbridge in the 1920s. During this period the GWR were involved in a legal battle to maintain their own passenger bus and road haulage operations. As insurance they started buying local transport companies, including the road haulage and passenger steamer operations of Southwood's N. March & Co. Ltd. The *Ilton Castle* and *Kenwith Castle* therefore passed to railway ownership but the *Ilton Castle* was laid up and never steamed again.

The *Kenwith Castle* at New Quay, Southville in the 1920s. Contrary to the postcard's caption, Kingsbridge Quay was further upstream, in Kingsbridge itself, which is visible in the background.

The *Kenwith Castle* approaching Kingsbridge in 1930. In the previous year the GWR had settled their passenger road transport dispute in the westcountry and amalgamated with the National Omnibus Co. Ltd to form the Western National Omnibus Co. Ltd, with buses running to Salcombe. The *Kingswear Castle's* days were therefore numbered and in 1932 she was sold to W. Worth of Calstock on the River Tamar.

The River Dart paddle steamer *Compton Castle* was employed in a static capacity as a café at Kingsbridge between 1964 and 1978, pictured by Bernard Cox. During this period she staked her claim to fame as the *Birds Eye Showboat* in television advertisements and her engine room was used in an episode of the television series *The Onedin Line*. She is currently used in a similar capacity at Truro – but little remains of the original steamer.

The last rowboat on the Portlemouth Ferry with ferryman Distin posing for photographer Edward Chapman. The ferry is still busy during the summer as it is easily the best way of reaching beaches on the coast shore opposite Salcombe.

Not a steamer or ferry in sight – and if you look closely neither is their any land. The people are entirely afloat on a massive raft of small boats, to view Salcombe Regatta. Little wonder therefore when so many people had access to so many boats, that visiting steamers were viewed more as a money making opportunity than as an excursion opportunity. A postcard by A.E. Fairweather of Salcombe.

The event is the Annual Wesleyan Chapel Sunday School treat from Aveton Gifford to Bantham, on south Devon's River Avon. The excursion craft is the local stone barge or lighter. Blissfully ignorant of Board of Trade rules and unaware of bye-laws they must have been breaking, the happy complement even invited messrs Balley and Flower of Dartmouth to produce this incriminating postcard of the event. To the song 'Yes we shall gather at the river', they floated downstream using the big sweeps to steer and a kedge anchor and chain (seen on the bow) to bring them safely to a halt at Bantham Quay. Part of the message on the reverse reads: '…you will see by the card that it is when we went to Bantham, can you own to those on the ship…'

Is it a ferry, tram or tractor? The title 'tractor ferry' seems to have been adopted for this singular vehicle crossing from Bigbury on Sea to the hotel on Burgh Island. At high tide the sea tram's 'stilts' are half submerged. This postcard shows the vehicle that was operating between the 1940s and 1969.

Five
Plymouth District

Previous Page: The *Princess Royal* steaming into Newton Creek with the River Yealm steamer *Kitley Girl*, partially obscured behind the paddler's funnel. The fishing boat is a Plymouth Hooker – i.e. a longliner for mackerel etc. The event is the Yealm Regatta when the creek's distinctive grey-back crabbing boats would be rowed in races.

The *Kitley Belle* of 1905, moored at Noss Mayo on the River Yealm. She was owned by George Hodge who ran a steamer service linking the villages of Newton Ferrers and Noss Mayo to the GWR's Yealmpton Branch, four miles upstream at Steer Point station. The Yealm was known to the maritime community as the Kitley River, because Kitley Quay was the highest navigable point.

The *Kitley Belle* in Newton Creek with the village of Noss Mayo in the background. Following the arrival of the railway at the nearby village of Yealmpton, Newton Creek developed as an desirable satellite of the Plymouth district and Hodge's steamer service prospered by providing the best link to Plymouth via Steer Point railway station.

The Steer Point steamer service suffered competition from new bus operations in the 1920s. The coal dispute and General Strike in 1926 forced the Hodges to convert the *Kitley Belle* to a more economical paraffin engine. The conversion proved disappointing and the Kelvin engined *Pioneer* was purchased from St Mawes as a replacement. She is pictured here at Steer Point in a postcard by Battershill's of Plymouth. The steamer service closed in 1929.

Extra work for Hodge's steamers was provided by visiting steamers from Plymouth. In this picture the Saltash, Three Towns & District Steamboat Co. Ltd's paddle steamer *Princess Royal* is anchored in the Pool of the Yealm with boats taking passengers off. The *Kitley Belle* is on the extreme right. She would take some passengers up to Steer Point for a return trip on the Yealmpton Branch.

Competition to the *Princess Royal* for the Yealm trade came in the shape of the opposing Millbrook Steamboat Co.'s paddle steamer *Hibernia*, which regularly shadowed the Saltash steamer. In this postcard the *Hibernia* is in the bottom of the picture, with the *Princess Royal* ahead, steaming up Newton Creek. The Yealm Hotel is on the left and on the hills above are some of the villas and houses which today cover the hillside.

The Saltash Three Towns & District Steamboat Co. Ltd's paddle steamer *Alexandra* at Kiln Quay in Newton Creek c.1910. The buildings on the quay were Lord Revelstoke's boat house and the quay served his estate, upon which Newton Ferrers and Noss Mayo stood. For a period before the First World War a tea garden was established near the quay and Saltash company steamers landed there.

Above: In 1910 the passenger fleet of the Saltash, Three Towns & District Steamboat Co. Ltd was amalgamated with the Plymouth Promenade Pier & Pavilion Co. Ltd and the company's name was changed to the Plymouth Piers Pavilion & Saltash Three Towns Steamboat Co. Ltd. For the sake of brevity, therefore, I shall simply call them 'Saltash' steamers.

Photographed one month before she was withdrawn from service in September 1927, the Saltash paddler *Alexandra* is pictured landing passengers by boat in the Pool of the Yealm. By the following winter she was lying at Cattedown, in Plymouth, being broken up.

Right: For many years Plymouth's excursion boats were required by the Board of Trade to be flush decked to visit the River Yealm – beyond the shelter of Plymouth Breakwater. Flush decked boats such as the Oreston & Turnchapel Steamboat Co. Ltd's *City of Plymouth* and the Millbrook Steamboat & Trading Co. Ltd's *Western Belle* were specifically designed for this purpose. After the Second World War, however, the rule was relaxed and for many years the Millbrook company's *Southern Belle* – with a forward well deck – maintained this daily afternoon trip. She is pictured entering the Yealm in the 1980s.

The Cattewater steamer *Swift* at the Oreston & Turnchapel Steamboat Co. Ltd's landing at Oreston. This company and their steamers provided a vital link for the south Devon villages of Oreston, Hooe and Turnchapel, to Plymouth across the River Plym. The water shown in this picture has since been infilled, almost to the height on the quay wall. The Cattewater is the name of the final reach of the Plym estuary.

Turnchapel *c.*1905. The windows of the houses in Borringdon Road face Plymouth across the water, while the sign points towards the easiest method of gaining the opposite shore. The steamers remained the best way of crossing to Plymouth, even outlasting the London & South Western Railway's branchline to Turnchapel.

Turnchapel Pier was built in 1889 for the sole use of the Oreston & Turnchapel Steamboat Co. Ltd's steamers. The *Swift* is alongside with two other steamers moored off the pier. In the background is the Mount Batten peninsula, where the steamers also made calls.

The *Rapid* on the beach at Turnchapel for maintenance. She was built in 1889 by Issac Darton of Mount Batten. Her non-condensing steam engines and boiler were supplied by Tangye of Birmingham. The helm shelter in the bow was fitted after the Second World War – until then helmsmen had no protection at all.

Oreston & Turnchapel Steamboat Co.
LIMITED

SUMMER TIME TABLE
(WEATHER AND CIRCUMSTANCES PERMITTING)

COMMENCING SATURDAY, JUNE 5th, 1954
Ferries Leave as follows—

MONDAYS to SATURDAYS until 11 a.m.

From Oreston for Turnchapel and Plymouth	From Turnchapel for Plymouth	From Phœnix Wharf, Plymouth for Turnchapel
A.M.	A.M.	A.M.
	6-30	6-45
	6-55	7-5
	7-20	*7-30
	7-50	*8-0
	8-25	8-35
	8-50	9-0 Oreston
9-15	9-25	9-35
	9-50	10-0
	10-25	10-35
	10-50	11-0
	11-25	11-35
	11-50	12-0 Oreston
P.M.	P.M.	P.M.
12-15	12-25	12-35
	12-50	1-0 Oreston
	1-10 W	1-20 W
1-15 NW	1-25 NW	1-35 NW
	1-30 W	1-40 W
	1-50	2-0
	2-10	2-20
	2-30	2-40
	2-50	3-0
	3-10	3-20
	3-30	3-40
	3-50	4-0
	4-20	4-30
	4-50	5-0
	*5-10	5-25
	5-35	5-45
	5-55	6-5
	6-25	6-35
	6-50	7-0 Oreston
7-15	7-25	7-35
	7-50	8-0 Oreston
8-15	8-25	8-35
	8-50	9-0 Oreston
9-15	9-25	9-35
	9-50	10-0

SATURDAYS from 11-20 a.m.

From Oreston for Turnchapel and Plymouth	From Turnchapel for Plymouth	From Phœnix Wharf, Plymouth for Turnchapel
A.M.	A.M.	A.M.
	11-20	11-30
	11-45	11-55
P.M.	P.M.	P.M.
	*12-5	12-20
	12-30	12-40
	12-50	1-0 Oreston
1-15	1-25	1-35
	1-50	2-0

Remainder of day as for Monday

SUNDAYS

From Oreston for Turnchapel and Plymouth	From Turnchapel for Plymouth	From Phœnix Wharf, Plymouth for Turnchapel
A.M.	A.M.	A.M.
	8-50	9-0 Oreston
9-15	9-25	9-35
	9-50	10-0 Oreston
10-15	10-25	10-35
	10-50	11-0
	11-10	11-20
	11-30	11-40
	11-50	12-5
P.M.	P.M.	P.M.
	12-20	12-30
	12-50	1-0
	1-20	1-30
	1-50	2-0 Oreston
2-15	2-25	2-35
	2-50	3-0 Oreston
3-15	3-25	3-35
	3-50	4-0 Oreston
4-15	4-25	4-35
	4-50	5-0 Oreston
5-15	5-25	5-35
	5-50	6-0 Oreston
6-15	6-25	6-35
	6-50	7-0 Oreston
7-15	7-25	7-35
	7-50	8-0 Oreston
8-15	8-25	8-35
	8-50	9-0 Oreston
9-15	9-25	9-35
	9-50	10-0

NW Not Wednesday   W Wednesday only
*CALLING AT MOUNT BATTEN

Extra Service from Turnchapel Weather permitting

By 1954 the Oreston calls had been reduced and there were only weekday morning and evening (worktime) calls at what was then RAF Mount Batten.

The Oreston & Turnchapel Steamboat Co. Ltd's *May Queen*, at Turnchapel Pier. She was built by Philip & Son Ltd of Dartmouth in 1946 and was the first on the company's Cattewater service to have a diesel engine – a four cylinder Lister. So pleased were the company's directors with the economies in operation, that they converted the *Swift* to diesel. She can be seen in her converted state approaching the pier. The *Swift's* origins went all the way back to the 1870s and she survived until wrecked in a storm in 1962 – although, like the apocryphal knife that had had three new handles and two new blades, there was little or nothing left of the original steamer by then.

One of the Oreston & Turnchapel Steamboat Co. Ltd's steamers turning off Plymouth's Phoenix Wharf, in Sutton Pool. Phoenix Wharf was built by Plymouth Corporation in 1895 and for the rest of the Oreston & Turnchapel Steamboat Co. Ltd's history was the Plymouth landing for their steamers.

The Saltash company's iron paddler *Eleanor*, on the right, leaving West Hoe Pier. Moored at West Hoe Pier is the Saltash company's steel paddle steamer *Alexandra*. Over at the Promenade Pier is the Millbrook Steamboat company's steel paddle steamer *Hibernia*. The Saltash, Three Towns & District Steamboat Co. Ltd owned West Hoe Pier, which resulted in the unfortunate situation where the premier steamboat company in the district was running in opposition to the Promenade Pier and whatever steamers it could attract. This situation was only resolved in 1910 when the Saltash and Pier companies amalgamated.

A busier scene at Plymouth's Sea Front Piers. From left to right at West Hoe Pier are the Saltash company's paddle steamers: *Alexandra*, *Princess Royal*, *Prince Edward* and *Empress* and the screw steamer *Albert*. At the Promenade Pier are the ex-Thames paddler *Brunel*, the *Hibernia* and just visible on the far side of the pier is the *Britannia*. The latter three paddle steamers all belonged to the Millbrook Steamboat Co.

The paddle steamer *Britannia* moored off Cremyll Quay, with the training ship HMS *Impregnable* in the background and Royal Navy apprentices maintaining a naval cutter on Cremyll Beach. Cremyll is in Cornwall, while Devonport – across the River Tamar – is now a part of the City of Plymouth. The *Britannia* was built by Philip & Son Ltd for John Parson's Millbrook Steamboat Co. She measured 63 tons gross, 75.3ft long x 16.1ft wide x 5.5ft deep. Her two cylinder compound diagonal engines were also built by Philips. Designed primarily to maintain passenger services from Millbrook Lake to Devonport, the paddler was also used as an excursion steamer running from Plymouth's Sea Front and the Devonport landing stages.

The Saltash company's *Alexandra* steaming down the Hamoaze – the deep and wide final stretch of the Tamar estuary.

The paddle steamer *Aerial* of the Saltash company was built in 1865 by Hedderwick of Govan, on the Clyde, for the Tamar & Tavy Steam Ship Co. Ltd. Originally she maintained market day services from the Tamar Quays to Devonport's North Corner pontoon on Devonport market days. She was later acquired by William Gilbert's Saltash Steamboat Co. (forerunner of the Saltash, Three Towns & District Steamboat Co. Ltd) and ran river excursions from Plymouth.

The Saltash racing gig *Beatrice* with the *Princess Royal* and other steamers of the Saltash fleet moored behind. This picture possibly dates from 1926 when the *Princess Royal* was laid up due to the coal dispute and the National Strike. She never entered service again and was broken up during the winter of 1927-1928.

The *Lady Ernestine* was the smallest paddler in the Saltash fleet, having been built to maintain steamer services on Millbrook Lake. Her shallow draught – around two feet – rendered her difficult to handle in the Hamoaze (she rarely visited Plymouth Sound). This feature proved useful, however, for trips to the shallow River Tavy and she was a regular caller at Lopwell Quay, where she is pictured *c.*1905.

The screw steamer *Devonia* was built in 1895 by Waterman's Yard at Cremyll (today Mashford's Yard). She was fitted with machinery from Plenty & Sons Ltd of Newbury. Although she helped out on the Millbrook steamer service, she was designed primarily as a river excursion boat, running from Plymouth and Devonport. Unfortunately the *Devonia* suffered badly from vibration while idling at landing places. It was so bad that passengers visibly trembled and little wavelets radiated from her quivering hull.

The steel paddle steamer *Hibernia* was built for the Millbrook Steamboat Co. in 1904 by Philip & Son Ltd. She measured 99 tons gross, 104.6ft long x 16.2ft wide x 8.25ft deep. Designed solely as a seasonal excursion steamer the *Hibernia* offered stiff competition to the arch rival Saltash company fleet.

The *Britannia* steaming under the new railway viaduct at Calstock which was nearing completion early in 1907. The Meccanno-like structure on the left is a wagon hoist, to lower wagons to the isolated quayside rails.

River Tamar, Calstock.

The ex-London County Council paddle steamer *Brunel* was the largest paddler ever to work on the river above Calstock. Her appearance in 1909 for the Millbrook Steamboat Co. was greeted with dismay by the Saltash, Three Towns & District Steamboat Co. Ltd. Within months of her arrival moves were made which led to the eventual amalgamation of the Saltash company with the Promenade Pier company – both of which were suffering financially. The *Brunel* was built by the Thames Iron Works in 1905 and measured 126 tons gross, 129.9ft long x 18.5ft wide x 6.7ft deep. She was purchased by John Parson for his Millbrook fleet for just £500. She is pictured in a Fred J. Paul postcard in the Calstock reach, steaming downstream.

Illustrating the grandeur of the River Tamar above Calstock, this S.B. Wadge of Tavistock postcard shows the *Britannia*, dwarfed by the towering Morwell Rocks, negotiating the sharp Impham Turn. The steam pinnace, nearest the camera, is full of passengers but remains unidentified.

Weir Head, the head of navigation on the Tamar, with the Saltash paddler *Alexandra* turning near the lock gates of the Tamar Manure Navigation. The straight cut of the navigation can bee seen behind the steamer, and the weir can just be made out as a line of white above the paddler's forward deck. The Tamar Manure Navigation comprised a five feet deep channel, extending from Morwellham Quay to a quay near New Bridge in Gunnislake (above the weir). The cut, in this picture, bypassed the weir and maintained the five feet depth in the reaches above. It was the canal company's unofficial abandonment of the navigation that led to the gradual silting of the river to Weir Head in the 1920s and has rendered such trips today as special spring tide affairs, perhaps only once a year.

The *Britannia* was the last of the Tamar paddlers to survive. She was withdrawn from service at the end of 1936 and scrapped in 1939 or 1940. She is pictured here on a Tamar excursion in the 1930s.

The *Western Belle* of 1936 was built to replace the paddle steamer *Britannia* for the Millbrook Steamboat & Trading Co. Ltd (as the Millbrook Steamboat Co. had become in 1929). She was a popular motor vessel in the Plymouth district for the next fifty years, a familiar sight on the rivers Yealm, Tavy and Tamar. She is pictured off Plymouth Hoe c.1965 en-route to Phoenix Wharf for a day's excursions.

The *Western Belle* in Sutton Harbour in the late 1940s – an unusual location for the motor vessel. Sutton Harbour has changed dramatically and is now a floating harbour with imposing lock gates instead of the friendly old harbour entrance. The fishing fleet is banished to Coxside – out of view to the right. The old fish market, on the left, is now a glassware retail outlet. The background is full of high rise waterside flats.

The *Southern Belle* was one of the prettiest passenger boats ever to ply in the Plymouth district. Built originally as the steamer *Shuttlecock* for the Cremyll Ferry in 1925, she was acquired by the Millbrook Steamboat & Trading Co. Ltd in 1945 when the company bought the Cremyll Ferry from the Mount Edgcumbe Estate. In the following year she was converted to Gleniffer diesel engines and had a top deck added.

The Turnchapel & Oreston Steamboat Co. Ltd's *May Queen* was purchased by the Millbrook Steamboat & Trading Co. Ltd in 1957, when the assets of the Cattewater steamboat company were being sold off. She entered service for the Millbrook company as the *Eastern Belle*. Ahead is the passenger launch *Lady Elizabeth* of 1927, built by Mashfords. She was the last boat built and owned by the Saltash company, designed originally to maintain trips to Weir Head, along the increasingly silted channel above Morwellham.

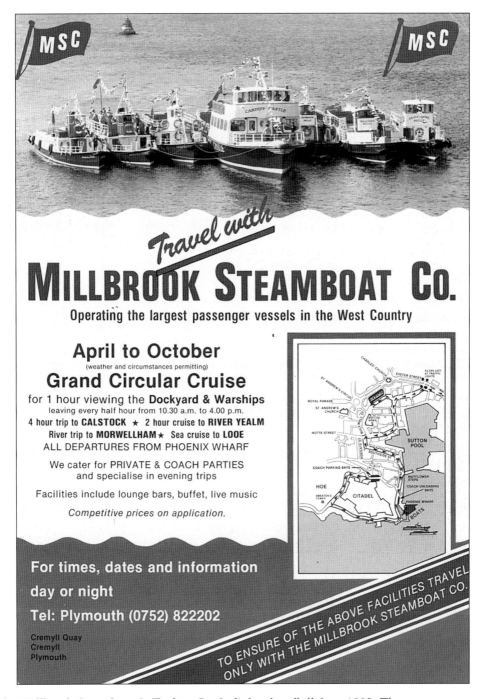

The Millbrook Steamboat & Trading Co. Ltd's last handbill from 1982. The company ceased trading in 1985. From left to right: *Northern Belle* – which has been on the Cremyll Ferry for three quarters of a century; *Southern Belle*; *Eastern Belle*; *Cardiff Castle*, *Plymouth Belle* – built by Mashfords in 1962; *Western Belle*; and *Edgcumbe Belle*. Today only the *Northern Belle* remains in the district.

The ex-River Dart Steamboat Co. Ltd's *Cardiff Castle* was acquired by the Millbrook Steamboat & Trading Co. Ltd in 1977. She is pictured here braving the sea outside the Breakwater, having been chartered for the start of the Transatlantic yacht race in 1985. In front is the Brixham trawler *Provident*.

A new generation of passenger boats filled the vacuum created by demise of the Millbrook Steamboat & Trading Co. Ltd. The most significant was the Mashford designed *Plymouth Venturer* of 1982. To some degree her appearance hastened the demise of the Millbrook company, as that company's new Dart based owners were not keen to endure competition from the *Plymouth Venturer*'s owners, Plymouth Boat Cruises Ltd of Millbrook.

Calstock remains as busy as ever, especially on weekend evenings. Most of these boats would have been chartered for parties, discos etc, all belonged to Plymouth Boat Cruises Ltd. From left to right: *Eastern Belle* – which was kept in Millbrook Steamboat & Trading Co. Ltd colours; *Plymouth Venturer*; *Plymouth Princess*; and *Totnes Castle*. The photograph was taken aboard the *Southern Belle* on a Friends of Morwellham charter trip to Weir Head in 1987.

The Cremyll Ferry and *Northern Belle* passed to the ownership of Tamar Cruising & Cremyll Ferry in 1984. Since 1987 they have also been running the 49 tons gross *Plymouth Sound* on river excursions from Plymouth's Sutton Pool.

By 1988 the number of boats touting for the Dockyard and Warship trade from Plymouth's Seafront seemingly began to outnumber prospective passengers. This sad decline in visitors came about partly due to negligence or arrogance on the part of Plymouth in presiding over the decline of its world famous Hoe and spectacular Seafront. Happily this state of affairs seems to have been realised and work is under way to reverse the situation. Pictured at the landing steps is the *Devon Belle* – ex-Millbrook Steamboat & Trading Co. Ltd. Moored at a buoy, waiting their turn are: the *Southern Comfort* (V.W. Bristow); *Westminster Belle; Skylark* (R.J. Elworthy); *Duke of Edinburgh* (K.J. Bridge); and the *Condor*. Moored alone is the *Argus*.

Left: Busier days in 1984 found the *Darthula II* (R.J. Elworthy) with a good load of passengers for a Dockyard and Warships trip. She is pictured off Cremyll in the mouth of the River Tamar.

Right: Each boat in turn on the Seafront's Dockyard and Warship trade sends a crewman to the top of the stairs to tout for business.

For a period from the 1970s a ferry service was run to Drake's Island in Plymouth Sound. The island was being leased to the Mayflower Trust for activity holidays and was open to the public. In conjunction with the Millbrook Steamboat & Trading Co. Ltd a ferry was run from Sutton Harbour and Cremyll Quay. The ex-Kingswear Ferry steamer *Humphrey Gilbert* was purchased for the ferry and renamed *Edgcumbe Belle*. She is pictured leaving the island's landing pier in 1983.

The liner tender *Sir Richard Grenville* of 1891 was the fourth unit of the GWR's tender fleet at Plymouth's Millbay Docks. This iron, twin screw, vessel was built by Laird Brothers of Birkenhead and measured 420 tons gross, 132ft long x 30.1ft wide x 12.6ft deep. She was regularly employed on sea excursions from Millbay Pier and Princess Royal Pier in Millbay, and would regularly be seen at ports between Falmouth and Torquay.

The ex-Mersey ferry paddle steamer *Cheshire* was purchased by the GWR in 1905 as something of a stop gap until their new twin sisters the *Sir Francis Drake* and *Sir Walter Raleigh* arrived three years later. In contemporary advertisements she was listed as running excursions, but was soon favoured as the main mail tender because her wide decks were ideal for continuing the mailbag sort before reaching the waiting mail trains at Millbay. She is pictured in the Inner Basin of Millbay Docks.

The *Sir Francis Drake* (nearest) and *Sir Walter Raleigh* at Princess Royal Pier in Millbay Docks. One hesitates to describe sister ships as identical – there is usually some difference – but decades of searching have revealed nothing obvious and they are impossible to distinguish from a distance. They were built by Cammel, Laird & Co. Ltd of Birkenhead in 1908 and measured 478 tons gross, 145.8ft long x 38.6ft wide x 14.1ft deep. The ships joined the *Sir Richard Grenville* and the *Smeaton* in the tender fleet, all were used on excursions.

In 1929 the GWR took delivery of their largest ever tender, the *Sir John Hawkins*. She was built by Earles Shipbuilding & Engineering Co. Ltd of Hull and measured 930 tons gross, 172.5ft long x 43.1ft wide x 14.6ft deep. She replaced the old excursion favourite *Smeaton*. The *Sir John Hawkins* is pictured on her maiden arrival at Millbay.

Plymouth's Sea Front and Promenade Pier, pictured in the 1930s. The GWR's *Sir John Hawkins* has just steamed out of Millbay. At the pier are the passenger boats *Devon Belle* of the Millbrook Steamboat & Trading Co. Ltd and the *City of Plymouth* of the Oreston & Turnchapel Steamboat Co. Ltd. On the far left is Drake's Island and in the background Mount Edgcumbe Park, in Cornwall.

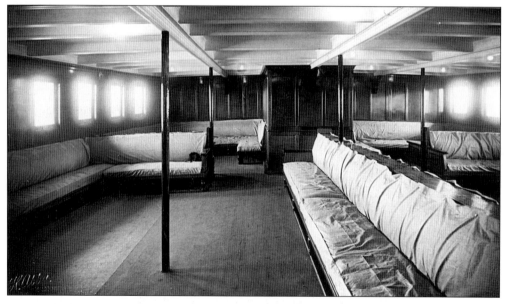

One of the benefits that Plymouth's excursion passengers enjoyed aboard the tenders was the high standard of passenger accommodation below deck. This comfort was not provided for the day trippers but for the well heeled ocean travellers from the liners at Plymouth, most of whom would be landing at night – timed so that the liner's final berthing at Southampton, Cherbourg, Le Havre etc would be in daylight. A novelty on an excursion might be to write your postcard in one of the writing alcoves provided, complete with brass wall light, ink well and stationery drawer. The saloon of the *Sir John Hawkins* is pictured prior to her delivery in 1929, the upholstery still protectively covered.

The last tender to be built for the liner trade at Plymouth was the *Sir Richard Grenville*, which effectively replaced her earlier namesake in 1931. She was built by Earles Shipbuilding & Engineering Co. Ltd and measured 896 tons gross, 172.5ft long x 42.1ft wide x 14.7ft deep. She was a sister ship to the *Sir John Hawkins* but unlike the sisters *'Drake* and *'Raleigh*, the *'Hawkins* and *'Grenville* looked very different, mainly because the latter steamer was oil fired with a much shorter elliptical funnel. She is pictured in the 1950s, moored at Princess Royal Pier pontoon.

Left: The General Saloon of the *Sir Richard Grenville*, with upholstery still partially covered prior to delivery.

Right: The decor of the *Sir Richard Grenville* was very cosy. If the interior design of liners like the *Bremen* and *Normandie* can be compared to the art-deco decor of Odeon cinemas, then the *'Grenville's* was music hall or Gaumont cinemas – with wood panelling, polished brass, railway rep upholstery, stained glass and white canvas stair edges. Pictured is part of her Smoking Saloon.

STEAMER EXCURSIONS

Weather and other circumstances permitting.

From PLYMOUTH

SAILINGS, DAYS, TIMES, etc.

JULY and AUGUST

from MILLBAY PIER, G.W. DOCKS

DAY	TO	Leave Millbay Pier	Arrive	Depart	Arrive Millbay Pier	Return Fare
JULY		pm	pm	pm	pm	s. d.
Wednesday, 25th	LOOE	2 15	3 30	7 45	9 0	5 0
	FOWEY	2 15	4 45	6 30	9 0	7 0
Thursday, 26th	EDDYSTONE	6 30	—	—	9 0	5 0
Tuesday, 31st	LOOE	2 15	3 30	7 45	9 0	5 0
	FOWEY	2 15	4 45	6 30	9 0	7 6
AUGUST						
Wednesday, 1st	LOOE	2 15	3 30	7 45	9 0	5 0
	FOWEY	2 15	4 45	6 30	9 0	7 0
Thursday, 2nd	EDDYSTONE	6 30	—	—	9 0	5 6
Monday, 6th	LOOE	am 10 0	am 11 15	7 45	9 0	5 0
	FOWEY	10 0	pm 12 45	6 30	9 0	7 0
	DODMAN POINT	10 0	—	—	9 0	12 0
	LOOE	pm 2 15	3 30	7 45	9 0	5 0
	EDDYSTONE	2 15	—	—	9 0	7 0
Tuesday, 7th	LOOE	am 10 0	am 11 15	7 45	9 0	5 0
	FOWEY	10 0	pm 12 45	6 30	9 0	7 0
	EDDYSTONE	10 0	—	—	9 0	12 0
	SALCOMBE	pm 3 15	5 15	7 0	9 0	7 0
Wednesday, 8th	LOOE	2 15	3 30	7 45	9 0	5 0
	EDDYSTONE	2 15	—	—	9 0	7 0
Thursday, 9th	LOOE	2 15	3 30	7 45	9 0	5 0
	FOWEY	2 15	4 45	6 30	9 0	7 0
Tuesday, 14th	LOOE	2 15	3 30	7 45	9 0	5 0
	EDDYSTONE	2 15	—	—	9 0	7 0
Wednesday, 15th	EDDYSTONE	6 30	—	—	9 0	5 0
Thursday, 16th	LOOE	2 15	3 30	7 45	9 0	5 0
	FOWEY	2 15	4 45	6 30	9 0	7 0
Tuesday, 21st	LOOE	2 15	3 30	7 15	8 30	5 0
	EDDYSTONE	2 15	—	—	8 30	7 0
Wednesday, 22nd	LOOE	2 15	3 30	7 15	8 30	5 0
	FOWEY	2 15	4 45	6 0	8 30	7 0

Children under three years of age, free; three and under fourteen years of age, half-fare.

REFRESHMENTS MAY BE OBTAINED ON BOARD.

The fares do not include the Looe Pier toll of 1d. per passenger, or the boat hire of 6d. each way at Looe, or 3d. each way at Fowey and Salcombe.

Plymouth passengers have the option of returning by rail from Looe on payment of 1s. extra, or from Fowey on payment of 6d. extra, on surrender of return portion of Looe or Fowey Steamer Ticket to the Booking Clerk at Looe or Fowey Railway Stations respectively.

Enquiries regarding Steamer Excursions should be addressed to the Dock Manager, G.W. Docks, Plymouth.

By the late 1950s the tender's cruising season was down to four weeks during the peak summer holidays. Subject of concern are those poor souls stuck in Looe between 11.15 a.m. to 7.45 p.m. on 6 and 7 August.

The *Sir Richard Grenville*, nearest, and the *Sir John Hawkins*, pictured on a summer's evening in the 1950s by Ivor Ireland. They are moored at Princess Royal Pier pontoon. The launch alongside the '*Grenville* is the *Argus* – the Port Health Authority launch, which also attended homebound liners.

Left: Pictured by Michael Doherty aboard the *Sir Richard Grenville's* 'final' excursion to the Eddystone Lighthouse on 9 August 1963, organised by Plymouth Chamber of Commerce. A hastily organised second final excursion took place on 4 September 1963, a special charter to the Eddystone Lighthouse by local cruising stalwarts.

Right: Following closure of Millbay's passenger and mail facilities in 1963, the *Sir Richard Grenville* was sold to Guernsey Lines Ltd to maintain passenger services between the Channel Islands and France. She was altered for her new career by Willoughby Bros Ltd in Millbay and emerged as *La Duchesse de Normandie* in which guise she is pictured here — looking a bit of a mess with all the extra deck clutter. She was eventually laid up in Millbay and sold for scrap in 1969.

The principal function of the tenders was to attend liners, their excursions were of secondary importance to the GWR – more of a fortunate perk. In this picture the GWR's *Smeaton* is attending Norddeutscher Lloyd's *Kaiser Willhelm der Grosse*, homebound from New York in 1906.

Liner passengers were important because they generated revenue for the railway. Mailbags were more important because they generated Post Office subsidies for the tenders, docks and the railway. Plymouth, or more precisely Millbay Docks, was the British mailport stipulated in most shipping line contracts owing to its strategic position at the entrance of the English Channel. Here mailbags are being loaded into a GWR Mail Storage Van at Millbay's Trinity Pier.

The P&O's *Ranchi*, (homebound from India) pictured from the deck of either the *Sir Francis Drake* or the *Sir Walter Raleigh*. The liner is moored in Cawsand Bay and passengers will disembark down the precarious looking gangplank. For their trouble they will be home long before the *Ranchi* reaches London – her final destination. P&O were required to stop at Plymouth because, although the India, Australia and Far East mail had proceeded overland from the Italian port of Brindisi, they had to land the Gibraltar mail.

One of the ships which provided good custom in the 1950s was the *Venus* of the Bergen Line, which in the winter months was picking up and landing cruise passengers at Plymouth at three day intervals, to and from Madiera and Tenerife. Reproduced is the cover of a programme from February 1956.

Aboard the *Sir John Hawkins* at Millbay, prior to joining the *Venus* in Plymouth Sound.

Halcyon days – passengers aboard a tender in Plymouth Sound head out to embark aboard either: the *Venus* for Tenerife or Madeira; or the Blue Star Line's *Uruguay Star* (centre) for South America. On the right is the Union Castle Line's *Durban Castle* or *Warwick Castle* – homebound on the Round Africa service.

The usual suspects – Cosens & Co. Ltd's *Alexandra* going astern from Princess Royal pontoon in Millbay Docks, during her 1920s incursion along the south Devon coast, boasting, it must be admitted, a good complement of passengers. The tenders are, left to right: the *Sir Walter Raleigh*, *Sir Francis Drake*, and at Millbay Pier the *Sir Richard Grenville* (of 1891). Note the two balls (black wicker spheres about three feet in diameter) hoisted on the signal mast at the end of Millbay Pier – this warned of a ship leaving the docks. One ball signalled that a ship was coming in.

P&A Campbell Ltd's *Westward Ho* looking for gainful employment in 1932 or 1933, entering Millbay Docks. She lasted the visitor's standard two seasons – i.e. one poor season and the second even worse.

The paddle steamer *Duke of Devonshire* had a brief stint in Ireland before returning to south Devon in 1936 in the ownership of Alexander Taylor. She is pictured with a good load, during this period, at Princess Royal pontoon, with the *Sir John Hawkins* at the pontoon and the '*Drake* or '*Raleigh* at Millbay Pier.

Maintenance of the *Duke of Devonshire* was undertaken in Willoughby Bros dry dock in the Inner Basin of Millbay. As there are no passengers aboard in this picture, taken by Graham Farr *c*.1937 off West Hoe, one hopes she is returning to Torquay after just such a visit.

From 1900 until 1908, when the new tenders *Sir Francis Drake* and *Sir Walter Raleigh* arrived, redundant units of the GWR's Weymouth based Channel Islands steamer fleet were tried out at Plymouth. The *Antelope* arrived in 1903 and worked as a tender and excursion ship until 1906. She is pictured in Millbay Docks by Frank of Plymouth.

In 1907 the GWR experimented with their ex-Weymouth steamers by running cross-channel trips to Jersey for the Battle of Flowers and to the Brittany port of Brest. The *Antelope* is pictured at Brest, possibly on her first trip. These visits resulted in a regular cargo service being instituted between Plymouth and Brest.

After gaining extra Parliamentary powers in 1909, to run regular French passenger services, the GWR bought the steamer *Chelmsford* from the Great Eastern Railway. Suitably renamed the *Bretonne* she is pictured entering Millbay Docks in 1911 – her only season. These cross-channel ventures predated Brittany Ferries by over fifty years, but elements that led to the establishment of today's cross channel ferry company were evident in these earlier enterprises.

The 1911 timetable for the *Bretonne's* Brest service.

Brittany Ferries' *Cournouailles* leaving Plymouth for Roscoff in 1984. She was purpose built in 1977, operating from a link span in Millbay Docks which had been built in 1972-1973. Brittany Ferries' services commenced in 1973 with the ferry *Poseidon*.

The 7,927 tons gross *Quiberon*, ex-*Nils Dacke*, leaving Millbay in 1989. She was initially chartered for Brittany Ferries' Santander and Cork service in 1982. In 1985 the ferry company bought her and she became a familiar sight at Plymouth.

The *Tregastel*, ex-*Njegos*, entering Millbay Docks in 1985. She was chartered in 1985 for the Roscoff route but transferred to Portsmouth in 1988.

The *Bretagne*, pictured leaving Millbay Docks, was launched in 1989 and joined Brittany Ferries' Spanish service at Plymouth. At 22,250 tons, she is larger than many of liners the old GWR tenders attended. Millbay today handles far more passenger traffic than it ever did in the days of the *'Drake*, *'Raleigh*, *'Hawkins* and *'Grenville*.

The Kingswear Railway Ferry steamer *The Mew*, looking very neat, but laid up in 'Death Row' in the Inner Harbour of Millbay Docks in October 1954. She was sold for scrapping in the following year.

The Devon Dock Pier & Steamship Co. Ltd's Tor Bay ferry steamer, *King Edward*, awaiting scrapping at Vicks Bros (Metals) Ltd's scrapyard in Stonehouse Lake, Plymouth, *c.*1936.

The *Waverley* in Millbay Docks in 1982. Coastal excursion opportunities on the south Devon coast today are virtually limited to occasional calls by the paddle steamer *Waverley* or the motor ship *Balmoral*.

Plymouth Hoe pictured from the stern of the *Waverley* in June 1984, en-route to Falmouth and Lizard Point. Such have been the changes on Plymouth's waterfront in recent years, that it is becoming increasingly difficult to find a suitable berth for the *Waverley* and *Balmoral*. Thankfully, however, excursions on the Exe, Dart and Tamar, trips across the bay in Tor Bay, and most of the ferry crossings in this book – working from long established landings – are still readily available and look set to continue for many years to come.